BARTER WITHIN THE BARK OF TREES

First Will & Testament
Poems Of Aging And Memory

LATIF HARRIS

©2015 Latif William Harris

All rights reserved. No part of this book may be reproduced or transmitted in any form or by any means including photocopy, recording, electronic, or retrieval system without written permission from the author or publisher.

Cover Photo "Heart in the Redwood" © 2014 by Alpha G. Gardner
Cover design by Lenore Goodell
Layout and Prepress by Luz Decker

ISBN 9780915008179-14-00 Paperback

ISBN 9780815008001-40-00 Hardcover

Library of Congress Control Number: 2015935585

Harris, Latif William
1940-
Poetry, Buddhism, Aging, Memory

SCOTT STREET DISTRIBUTOR
2261 Market Street #310
San Francisco, CA 94114

Also available on Amazon.com

PREFACE

I began writing poems at the age of twelve and found my way to North Beach in 1959 when I was 18 years old. Met most of the poets who made up the San Francisco Renaissance and "Beat" movements then in full swing. I met the great artist Robert LaVigne who was then painting a huge show and designing sets and costumes for the Actors Workshop. He was originally Peter Orlovsky's lover but when Ginsberg came on the scene he became Peter's life long partner. LaVigne taught me so much. He introduced me to John Wieners' *HOTEL WENTLY POEMS*, which I still consider to be one of the best books of poetry ever written. His natural lyricism pulling personal and historic events into this group of poems written in the period of a single week touched the marvelous.

In 1965 I participated in the huge Poetry Conference at U.C. Berkeley where I met Robert Creeley, and decided to move to New Mexico to study with him at U.N.M. After finishing undergraduate work, Creeley recommended me for a Graduate Fellowship to the University of Essex in England where I studied in 1968/1969. I spent the next two years traveling and living in European and Near Eastern countries. Some of the poems in this book were written in an earlier time. However. the long Second Section was written in the preceding year or so. I looked back over my work and found poems that presage so many future events that led to *Barter Within The Bark of Trees*, which is the last line of the poem in Section One.

I was the founding editor and publisher of the iconic letterpress literary and graphics magazine *ANTE* in Los Angeles 1963-1964.

My first chapbook was published by Larry Goodell's DUENDE PRESS in New Mexico 1965. I have had 11 chapbooks published and one nationally distributed book *Bodhisattva's Busted Truth* from Browser Books, San Francisco in 2006, now in 2nd printing.

I spent three years putting together a mammoth anthology of Beat and S.F. Renaissance poets and those who were in some way influenced by these movements internationally. Beatitude was a mimeographed magazine started by Bob Kaufman, Bill Margolis and John Kelley in North Beach 1959. In 1960 City Lights Publishers published a collection of these sheets. With the help of friend Neeli Cherkovski, John Landry and Michael Rothenberg we put out the word and slowly hundreds of manuscripts poured in resulting in: *BEATITUDE GOLDEN ANNIVERSARY 1959-2009* © Latif Harris 2009, ISBN 978-0-615-29394-3 (paperback) 552 pages including 111 page reprint of City Lights 1960 Edition; First Printing 1000 copies.

Though I do not consider myself a "Beat" poet, my youthful connection to poets like Jack Spicer, Robert Duncan, Robert Creeley and the Black Mountain poets, I was drawn to the general movement referred to incorrectly as the "Beat Movement." I feel very deeply that the brilliant Jack Kerouac is the one and only "Beat" writer and what followed is rightly called the Jack Kerouac School. Certainly Kerouac's poetry, which is not being read like his novels, contains the spiritual depth of "beatitude" as described in his journals. One of the best poems of the generation is the Song of The Sea at the end of his Big Sur novel. What he attempted in that masterful piece of writing and to have a beatific realization at its completion is a standard by which I measure my work.

I was involved in the activity that swirled around the City during the 50th anniversary celebrations of the Six Gallery Reading where Ginsberg first read *HOWL*, Kerouac's *ON THE ROAD* and the *Beatitude Golden Anniversary*. I was giving many readings as one of the "survivors" of movements, which made San Francisco the poetry capital of the U.S. The energy from these events led to the writing of this book, an ongoing open-ended poem (what Jack Spicer called the "serial" poem) of memory and aging.

I have stayed true to my ethic of a natural occurring technique in the surrealism and the development of first thought best thought in Zen. There is a term in Tibetan Buddhist teachings called "rang-bop" that means ever flowing, and I have thought of my work as a whole as ever flowing.

FORWARD

"Titanloose" is what I call Latif Harris' poetry. A play on a titan among us and at the same time a writing that's "tight" and "loose", the former in the sense that, as a child of the atomic age and the buddhistic graces that came to American poets therefrom, he has mastered the precision of images in relation to his feelings---as he has in-breathed the meaning of Joycean interior monologue---and loose because underlying much of this book is a rhythmically jazzy notation making sound-bridges allover the pages. It is that unspoken immediacy of idiom that transcends both his age (and aging) and memory of human tragedies and brings more than the poet himself to live again, upheld.

The poetry of Latif Harris contains his lifelong serious involvement with Buddhism and death as the heart of the art of the transient journey to the beginning where the end has already been out lived. This makes for a very mortal, both confessional and consoling. And in measures that are various, but always with a strong feel for structure, and in that sense, faithful to the classics, no matter the surface ease of his 'californial texturing'. There is hardly a single poem in his work that is not a praise-song received from his wisdom-school studies on the path.

--Jack Hirschman
Poet Laureate San Francisco
Emeritus

Table of Contents

PREFACE Latif Harris	i
FORWARD Jack Hirschman	iii
One Morning	1
Anti Objects	2
How About Tuesday Around Midday	12
The Gift I Give	13
Bridge 'N Memory	14
At the Door	15
Stone Renga Cycle	16
Notes of Blue Sage	17
Coyote Seen	18
Icons of Repair	20
Untitled	30
Untitled	31
Everyday Dream	32
SECTION TWO NOTES	34
Barter Within the Bark of Trees	35-81
AFTERWORD	iv
A NOTE FROM THE EDITOR	vi
BOOKS BY AUTHOR	vii

ONE MORNING

& so there we sat
  high on dharma

& telegraph hill
  talking of death

& moldy leaves
  & wind & tugboats
  & watching Berkeley

bare a new sun
 brilliant & naked
  re-planning yesterday

& forgetting today
 an impossible task
  & walking back down to earth

& waking up with them
 in the streets on streetcars
  & riding through the day

& forgot the beginning
 & it became yesterday
  as will tomorrow
   & next week
    & forever

                              North Beach 1961

ANTI-OBJECTS

> For Gordon Wagner's "Half Way to Infinity"
> Vorpal Gallery, 1979

1

Who returns from the sea
whispering compositions
salted skin and
watery eyes

The sun is alive in its pink
and orange splendor
at the savage moment it
drops behind the flat sea

He falls into a lush wilderness
where love survives like
a lost tooth
among the bleached bones
in the dark green sea

Among the torpedoes and
shark fins

He is high and would
stay that way forever
slipping in among the mollusks
held together by a thin silver thread

He would take his place
in the lining of this poem
Between the conical breasts
of the woman he loves

2

Alongside his brothers
defying the executioner

The net of his death
thrown out into the sea
to snare the living

Spits back the bitter seed

He is bored and moves
from room to room
his slow rhythms are not cool
he walks back and forth
      stumbling
on the slick cables of
      loneliness
he is lazy
drugged by
  a rugged silence
not crazy
but iced

Only love
    in its speechlessness
will save this man's life

analogs of feeling tumble into the work
  his hands long to hold
      a woman's slim waist

Once again
    in the finger paintings
of his mind
    it all turns brown

3

Watery eyes
        blue
as ink spilled on glass tables

squares
        of obsidian and ivory
circles
        of roses and fallen fruit
lemon
        and alabaster
and horns from the rhinoceros

thumbprints
        and braided hair

electromagnetic solar winds
filling the basket of the aurora borealis

Antiobjects like rocks' bottoms
        sitting ten thousand years
                inside the poet's mind

4

Monarch butterflies
           it is September

we learn of Saturn's rainbows
the music
      is not grey today

images walk the lines of my friend's face
           onyx outshines the diamond

the world cannot be modern again
      it does grow older

was the lilac of love songs
danced to on piers near the sea

green sea or grey sea
the palace burning
      in the palm of my hand
is her breast

the orchestra has played here before
        we are dancing to the roar
              of our memory

5

Legs are nothing more
                than tails
in the amniotic sea

and arms the wings
pulling us through the air

the cold night trains between Milano and Paris
make trades of life

snow falling on frozen iron
iced windows and steam
a small fire built in the palm
                of your living hand
narrow the pupils of my eyes

time passes slowly
                as tortoises
on their way to Bimini

we are high and the Swiss towns
freeze more deeply
they could almost turn yellow
as the Pernod

while the smooth terrain of your body
fills my lungs
                with tropical air

6

The rutile cracks in her pampered lips
like the restlessness of ladies
who row rented boats

rise up in the pallor of ducks eyes
pressed out against the surprised

evenings

we catch ourselves falling
in tumblers beside the fire
she lifts an eye
       like an oar
struck by Phoenicians

7

Her arms unroll
    the solid ocean
in a box of toothpicks

salted pearls
        become her afternoons

against the blue porcelain barriers
her fixed eyes are granite
on which the carved world slumps

on which the carved world slumps
like
    severed fingers

8

Following minds
red shadows of flesh hang entwined among the flowers

heroic bodies fall like embers
below a rain of arrows
ashes trapped between layers of ice
are raised like flags
                of blue diamonds

You are alive
        far from the passions that raised the old flame
where the voice
of a woman rules

She ruled all that was delicate
all the froth within the deep grottos of desire
        ember and ice and release

You are alive
        among the organs of memory
where the voice of a woman rules

9

The remote owl calls
to unresolved oceans

I swim unmolested
beneath the lids
of your closed eyes

the delicate canopies
of sleep
        ripple along your lips

down into grottos
of the fractured iris
into the blue green
golden brown light
        like a plunging Phoenix

I will break the seals
of red wax

walk on the tips of urchins
        with bare feet

to reach the opened clams
grazing in your dreams

10

How severe is the sound of a voice
above the ocean

how sleek the wild cats that roam
among the rocks
hunting small prey

like the loneliness a man is left with
at the end of a day

effigies hang in the spray
like the bones of tortoises

Albion, Albion
      what name must be created
to sabotage the hillside lore

whose voice
      can be heard
           above the roar

HOW ABOUT THURSDAY AROUND MID DAY

How fragile the flesh and bone
rubbing against the imagination
of the moment

holding all memory
in the quick tap dancing
of afternoons passing

listening to the sounds
of infinity
dressing for the day

Dexter Gordon blows cool
at midnight Keystone Corner

leave to meet you
quarter passed eleven

feel so full of myself
think it must be heaven

THE GIFT I GIVE

Do not become bound
by hopes and fears
regarding this practice
we call life
                and death

effortlessness is the key
not accomplishment
through practice
                and head banging

give up your attachment to all
but the view
and then
                give that away too

BRIDGE'N MEMORY

Memory like history
is a fiction existing
in the nothingness
                  of the past

yet the mind of music and poesy
like fugitives flee
                  from the past

flooding my imagination
as my aging

becomes a kind of play ground
of degeneration
and the mind
                  a fugue
of exquisite confusions

the moments sliced
by a mirror
                  shattered
into hypnogogic shards
of a billion reflections
thrown down
                  by the sun
which still warms
my old body

and in each moment
I explore the reflections
like a Bodhisattva
becoming a Bridge
of lingo
                  letting them
pass over me

AT THE DOOR

In the Square near Kensington
where lilacs profuse
near the roses

a knock from the knocker
then a bell

it is time to gather
two pints of milk
on the stoop
with cream
          floating on the top

for Camille and the Baby Simon

in the midst of civil kindness
a tradition
          not yet broken

                            London 1969

STONE RENGA CYCLE

For Neeli

The stone thrown into the air
is still for a moment
like a kite or kitten

In all things there is stillness
I am at times
in meditation still

Before the wild horses
of my mind take over
nothing will stop them

Pebble or boulder also find
that moment when rolling stops
cleverness changes nothing

NOTES OF BLUE SAGE

Recognized it at the Timbuktu Trail
flying eagles and One Eyed Jacks
north of the twin peaks

atop the adobe Kiva
when my ochre bones
are done to dust

let them whip it up
like a lovers lust
like the sun's splash at dawn
in the Great River
refreshing us at New Buffalo

nude each morning
light of the male sign
penetrating the Rio Grande
urging up from the cold well
of civilization

a bell sounds
we eye the vestibule
of a very high desert

COYOTE SEEN

As space curves
it must eventually come back
to meet itself

wherever it began
it will also end
which is back where

it begins again
coming upon that coyote
alongside the wet mountain road
with it's heavy silver-gray winter coat
slicked by
        s
       n
        o
       w
                f
               l
                a
                k
                e
               s

        we know we must meet him again
at this same spot
at the end of that
    l
     o
      n
       g

```
    S
      L
     O
       W


     c
    u
    r
     v
       e
```

Just as the light bends
traveling with us
        like the headlights of the car

minus its speed
            striking coyote's eyes
it reflects back hitting our eyes

and I know with certainty
all those things
        we've seen together
will repeat over and over
no matter how deeply
or in what shade
            death shall finally freeze us

ICONS OF REPAIR

"It is not enough to cover the rock with leaves
We must be cured of it by a cure of the ground
Or a cure of ourselves,
That is equal to a cure of the ground,
A cure beyond forgetfulness
The fiction of the leaves is the icon
Of the poem, the figuration of blessedness
And the icon is the man."
— Wallace Stevens

1

There are memories that lactate
through the eyes
behind the eyes
brimming with icons
of former lives

like light sealed in fossils
within a damp ancient wall
leaking out around the edges

it is the color of milk
seen through a thin slice of white opal
he turns his head

slightly to the right
and sees the messages
tooled in Paleolithic rock

his head like a hammer
strikes the pillow
with the first rays of dawn

2

It is upon him

like an endless flight of mallards
stretching along all the days of Autumn
over the tulip fields of Holland

it is upon him
with more power than ever before
it reaches down through him
like very slow motion lightning
kicking on the stars

it is upon him
like an answer to the question
he had ceaselessly recomposed
walking with the hands of his sons
held tightly within his own

it is once again upon him
like feinting into strength
leaving a meaningful trail of shadows
whose imprints are valleys of commerce
valleys of trees and rock
valleys of sand moved by wind
valleys he has walked

holding tightly the repetition of lines
in the palms of his children's hands
the lines he passes from his father
and all the fathers that stretch back
like an endless flight of mallards
stretching along all the days of Autumn
over the tulip fields of Holland

3

His disillusions began unwinding
like a wrapper around common coins

he held his head up
and yelled at demons traveling
unconcerned through the house of dreams

where is the roof he cried

these libraries
        these broken
                mechanical things
these crawl spaces
hallways and marble stairs
these precious and wholesale episodes
are dingy

where is the roof he cried
the light the air the distant blue stars
this house is a suicide note
a trembling flyleaf in an open book

where is the roof he cried

4

He played certain overtures
on the strings
           of his strength of youth

sometimes disguised as a swan
at others
      an armed demon
he wrapped and repelled
           until
he became both full and empty

then divining the mood of the crowd
like a minstrel
        moved on
the dream began to bend
back on itself
repeat itself through slick contours

5

Within himself
        soft armor pierced
by the morning wind

she bends over him
            singing
the loons along the bank
watch the colored balls sink
one by one
            into the mossy pockets

of the green felt lagoon

the prehistoric wizard
        with the eyes of a shark
the lizard
        in a suede suit
stands waiting
        for his shot

6

He wore his animal skins
until he wore
           the animals thin

wearing down all things
              he could not otherwise
                      control

sometimes for pride alone
did he drop a large chested buffalo

then in thundering herds
drove them from the plains for good

having leveled the living top
he drilled below into the living past

pulling up the liquid fern and flesh
and firing it once again
put on ancient animal skin

7

By the poet
days dull and sharp as a thorn
beneath a yogi's rock seat

admonishing clusters of wasps
swarm above his head

he loiters in the mechanics of night
you can see him limping
              along darkened streets

or striding high moonlit mountains

how many times does he turn
at the moment of pleasure
to deeper darker thoughts

toward the ultimate dark door
framed in opal light

he feels in all pleasure
              a sudden gasp of doom

he sometimes lies frozen
within the small tributary of his life

like a giant headed carp
with black and gold eyes

8

Tapering down
engulfed in paper weights
his solid dreams
              of tropical medicines
harbored in the stomachs of eels

wind blows up the corners of uniformity
psychiatric concerns ramble
              like flicked eyes

flames purse their lips defiantly

in the critique
of his fantastic mind

in the basement of scientific tomes
Blake hands him a large and heavy key

razzle-dazzle tics and foot tapping
              arched his back and smiled

9

Losing track of dates
      like hoof beats

comforted by the blue springs
centered in a small circle of green

mathematics spring up here
in conversation among camels

he passes through many lands
in search of his own face
listening
      listening

salaams and goodbyes

he sits in crowds
beneath the folded flaps
of empty tents

he is no great man
sitting beside the weathered bent men
arriving hollow eyed

from long journeys
through the numbing passion of their lives

he sits among them like a crystal
vibrating

among them as a traveler
      listening

10

He activates the sky
with copper rods
now absorbing the shock
           like waves of delight

small puffs of cloud
crisscross the eyes
like backbones curving
in the solid sleep
of the deep

like an x-rayed bank
of dozing crocodiles
on the blue sands of the Ganges

four sharp jolts

before the heart loosens
and falls from the fourth floor
injuring several turbines
          passing below

listening
          once again
it is upon him
          upon him
once again

                    San Francisco
                    1979

UNTITLED

On the edge of obliteration
clouds white as sheets of lacquered chalk
reform the sky

me at the door that will not close
navigating through the human ritual
which will not close
mouth ajar

like a pelican's
just as it hits the water

standing by the door of your body
               opening and closing
defiant and uncertain
as solid space

is full and empty

desire comes and goes
               like Bedouins
traceless
     catafalques
        of passing days
          and places

perhaps yellow dried gardenias

still scented
         will call
     and time once again
will stand
       aside

                        Mendocino 1976

UNTITLED

It's the afterimages
lurking among the linen
at the soft periphery
of the bed clothes
where hindoos ply their trade

It's the green flash
after the red sun falls
behind the great metaphysical ocean
of blue cellophane

It's all alike
becoming a cloud filled doll
rolled in sesame scrolls

                        S.F. 1984

EVERYDAY DREAM

I have been visiting the worlds
between sleep and awakening
the worlds of vapor trails
and watermelons
salt air and acacia
where intellect surrenders to curiosity
all her rigid demands

sounding of a soft hammer
against a bell
a bell which will not sound
a bell whose resonance
resides in the dawn

I have been visiting the worlds
of a thousand islands
strung together like beads
encircling the languid heart of a
leopard
which contains photographs
of distant planets
with violet mountains and orange skies

I have been out there so long
that maps have begun weeping

blistering noons
frozen in the rings of Bristlecone Pine
arboreal quills stopped in mid-air
like bolts of green lightning

Intransigent as a porcupine
yielding as a woman
made of water and air

invisible as the print of a sparrow's foot
on a frosted piece of white marble

I have been out there so long
that rescue has become unnecessary

the drone of helicopters has settled down
with the bees

the shouts of the rescue party
are drowned by the leaves

in the domain of morning
when activity replaces me

I will fall asleep
on a carpet of dark dreams

and barter within the bark of trees

SECTION 2

Notes On Typography and Phrasing

To read this text in the center justified form

think of each line as a phrase
as it comes

relax
do not read too rapidly
but slowly

let your breath
relax into each line
as your eye
shifts downward

do not anticipate anything

this work comes from the channels and vessels of my heart-mind

from a life of seventy four years

from dreams and illusions and visions
joys and sorrows
experiences of divine joy
and irrefutable Dharma

i decided to use a 14 pt. typeface for easy reading.

Latif William Harris
San Francisco 2014

Tears Are Words That Cannot Be Spoken

"No one listens to poetry"
 -*Jack Spicer*
Yes the Time is Half Full
Because I too could not stop for death
I turn to my forges of poetry for words
and phrases to stand on

my Blake's key handed to me directly
in a dream 1967
the year of a resurrection
lysergic fireworks
flowers and assassinations
roses in rifles

Shelley Keats Whitman
H.D. Paz Eluard
Nunzio of Greek bloods
Gregory Corso
my family of minds
mine the deep language in this time
thru this piccolo Momentos Intimos

Era of the Rough Beast
Kali Yuga Waltz

"Every disease is a musical problem"
 -*Re W.H. Auden*

> There are so many little dyings it does not
> matter which one you call death
> *-Re Kenneth Patchen*

> and nothing is final only parking lots
> *-Re Jack Spicer*

Facing emptiness I have day dreams in floods
falling asleep throughout the day

seeing into the emptiness of my aging
sometimes my playland
where I stand sit
then fall

onto my exhausted body of degeneration and the mind
rests in a fugue of exquisite confusion sliced by
melodies of memory

> The woods are lovely dark and deep
> but I have promises to keep
> and miles to go before
> *-Re Frost*

Erasure blends us forward
as what was there
has gone somewhere else
like dust blown
or else we surmise it so
what a surprise even though
we knew it would be so

and soon I will fall asleep
everything moving at light's speed
or beyond

I find myself
seeming feeble
but the View
is Perfection still

It felt so good
when we were there
children in love
driven
by wisdom and skill

Yab Yum
not quite

The thrill of fucking
waits awhile

We
wise beyond our years

me twelve and you but eleven
your little hairless mound

felt so smooth
breasts just budding

I remember you B
in bed playing
with our nameless parts

Mothers out getting ripped
after a day at the racetrack
leaving us in bed together
as baby sitters
for younger brothers

AFTER SOME YEARS

Youth felt so good when we were there beneath a
shower of rock & roll
in love
fucking
lit by the tail of a comet on the fields of flying so
high
A love supreme
Coltrane hums
ah hum ah hum a hum ah hum

you felt so cool with skin like silk
in my fading it is the same my love
somehow remembering still

the many forms my lovers took
how many impossible to know

only Woody Allen as Zelig escapes death
in the fins of my swimming
in the movies of disguises
and paralyzed by fear of dying
at Saturday afternoon flicks
as a kid
Three sons three brothers and three wives I've had
and nightmares about the lost ones
though they are long ago reborn
repairing broken Samayas
left to me

Sitting Inside
gazing
at the door
where the light
of days-end shines
I see question marks
encircled
by Bindus
I light
oil lamps
honoring
all
that senses

Born feet first on
New Years Eve 1940

The last year of the old world

Year of
The Iron Dragon/Mars in Scorpio
conjuncts my ascendant
my mind whirls

Erasure blends us forward
as what was there
has gone somewhere else
like dust blown
or else we surmise it so
what a surprise even though
we knew it would be so

what a surprise
even though
we knew it would be so
everything moving
at light's speed or more

I am feeble
but the View is perfect stillness
emptiness of space
remembering youth throughout
remembers the moment I am wrapped in now

A few miles from where I lived
in the little town of Waverley Hall Georgia
me recovering from Polio

remember Roosevelt's death
at Warm Springs

more wars come
my life of wars
continue
the Atomic Bomb paranoia
radio count down
like entertainment near Las Vegas

in LA. shaken awake by Mother
dragged outside to see
the fireball of atomic fusion
making two suns rise

The alchemists make deals with good and evil
at last
the alchemists
combined elements into
no gold
but massive death instrument of volcanic fire

this awful trick known in centuries past
the Alchemist seeking gold thru fusion
of lead and sulfur
hellfire and lightning
liquid silver

WHEN MY ALPHA APPEARS

at the end of one long life

and WE have been ONE for thirty four years

OMEGA awaits still

moments come go like Marlon Brando
Pocahontas and me
-Re Neil Young

In The Attics of my life
so stoned in our beautiful bodies
nude
wound in the grasses of Natchez Pass
New Orleans and mountains of the Great America
unbroken

broken mind holds to the odors of these places
where my semen dropped
eyes dazed
ears filled with Suzanne down by the river

I told you I was a wanderer with a heart set on the
next place
next woman
in this place unreal

Sometimes in the hollow air of Holland
art rises like funicularis into a Gothic cloud
where the bride and groom float with a fiddle and a
cow

Is this just my mind traveling faster than the speed
of light
what I saw the day some men landed on the moon

I am not in charge of your dog
does it sound familiar
my poems of sinew bone and heart
does it sound like
an infomercial to you

are you buying that stuff on TV
It's you who got you aced for nothing
masturbating
in your recliner

Take deep breaths then leave me alone I am tired
and old and out of breath moving closer to big back
door the feather duster of immortality
cannot brush you clean of the ultimate dust
collected in the cracks and folds of your living body
soon the door of this finality will open wide
poof you will shoot thru bang! the door will close

behind you
you are out of here
you might fall down you might feel bliss
I have no idea what will happen to you
I have no wisdom nothing to share with you

so many years in closets and garages
back seats of old automobiles

miles and miles
of motels
poverty and sick children wars and revolutions
impotence perpetuating evil
do not forget that everything is emotional
when you start unwinding
and all emotions are wisdomless like "Buddhahood
Without Meditation"
turns wisdom to emptiness
Refining Apparent Phenomena
in pure space
forget your breathing
count on nothing

was a time we were swimming in a river
near Utrecht so freely
travels in ancient countries
studying poems and buildings filling
architectural notebooks
fishing for sweet women
who would lay down with me in day dreams

I am falling down
in these days of the ending
trying to remember

Old Age is
just a pack of cards
thrown into a wind storm
and tears choke me with sorrow in a fog
of self pity

wordless
not hopelessness

but huge desires arise when we bathe in words
trying to unload all the sounds of my
morning dreams
leaking into the foggy canyons of my youth
waking into the dreams of dislocation
nothing is recognizable
a series of hallways are waiting chords on my arms
The Buddha teaches
making visits into so many dark closets will only
waste your days
there are fewer than more magic entanglements
become a circus when love bites
memories no
longer cease

The scales of the python peel away
dropping into the tannin dyed river
sun drops gold
the purest of colors on floating leaves
reflected in autumnal ochre and yellows
ripples of wind and mad bugs
ferry the eyesight down stream
Tie my chi to a tree
even though I am growing old
I still love rock and roll
jump up in my living room
and shake everything I've got left to shake.

Erasure blends us forward
as what was there has gone somewhere
like dust blown
or else we surmise it so
what a surprise even though
we knew it would be so

remembered in the root
of the human brain
aggression - rituals - and fear
swirl like a field of stars
and the yellow chromium Sun Flowers
Van Gogh's high-hat drums
beneath the showers
of crows

Magritte shaving
with smoke and mirrors
redoubling the oil of bird feathers
licked by conifers and claws

Whatever falls out
of me
lands here
nothing symbolic
can be remembered
only colors and shapes
these are the assumptions of realities
with which I greet this day

In these Sonoma canyons
the sulfur water's fog
smells not rotten
but soothing in my mouth
Saturn's child

phlegmatic she called me
when fire made me not wince
her exotic tattoos
turned me on
we made children

driving ever deeper into her
mysterium of lassos

long dark hair and seaweed brown eyes
flickering with emerald flashes

hooked me

oiled Mediterranean skin
covered by my Nordic self
blond Scots Irishman
back to
The Land of Enchantment
Placitas
invaded by hippies
Hog Farm visited
before Chicago
Larry and Ann

Ann who became witness
to big belly
shotgun wedding
at Kensington Registrar
not so long after
little did we know
never would we see her
be with her
again

Like Virginia Wolfe
she disappears into
the cold waters
off Brighton Beach

Jimmy Hendrix and Janis
so many died then

off we went her pregnant
only three moons of penetration
to Albion
on Icelandic Air

There is no nature
which is not a part of me
dust of stars from the edge
and beyond Dharmata
it was endless then

The holistic thunder of my heart
rumbling in my temples

as I fall asleep on the toilet
again

falling forward on my head
I hear the caws of crows
which come at dawn
to awaken the nesting birds
behind our 1885 Victorian
in hundred year old garden

likewise their cause
to wake me
still humped on blue and white
tiles

but becoming
yet

I try to prepare for continuation
rebirth
in a world changed
by Bodhicitta
simple kindnesses are still
at the bottom
deeply buried in our hearts
the hurricanes above
moves us not

My mind no longer mends
or bends so easily

events of the day
flow through this slough of time
in slow motion

appointments missed
forgotten

plasticity lost

on age worn cells of old films
will the work be lost so soon
will someone find these lines
yellowed and crisp like an old menu
or telephone bill

Memory

like history
is a fiction
existing in the nothingness
of the past
yet the mind still
likes
playing muscular images
pumping iron
like fugitives fleeing
the past flood
like my aging
becomes a playground
of degeneration
and the mind
a fugue of exquisite confusions

sliced by the moments

Yet it crossed my mind
to start sending new messages
instead of replying
to old ones

I did see that you had said
leave it as it is
but wanted to make sure
as it seemed

upon the weak grip
of memory
I have much to say
as H.D. had
in her declining times
"we meet in antithesis of kind"
at eighty she writes about her lust
re-awakens the Doges of Venice

Meter
Dr. Williams
said like
—oh them
gum balls tumble
from the penny
slot--

cola or soda

from the globe

our lingo

takes solos
and a bag of
salt peanuts

eaten like sacks of dactyls

When I went to see the etchings
of Blake
brought to my seat
in the British Reading Room
by a porter in white gloves
who stood behind
looking over
my every move

sitting in that circular temple of wisdom
where so many brilliant asses
had sat before me
and after
until they knocked it out
as if it had no permanent vibration
they fake you out
are not actual

their ideas without vision

entrance like a box office
of suburban stainless steel

Dr. Williams wrote poetic
prescriptions
in doctor scribble
with two emphatics
of double accents
and variable foot

from languages left
in Attica
spontaneous poetry with
rhyme
rhythms

DAY BY DAY IT SLIPS AWAY

Memory is devouring itself
(is such a thing possible)
I sit down
as moments shudder
is this a stick up
or an earthquake
falling away
into the illusions
hands in my head wind up
like dead clocks

as life itself spills out
slipping away

day by day
my eyes still see the light
billowing thru a window pane
wet with rain
floaters slide down like flies
on the white screens
of my vision
remembering what?

The afternoons I loved
like French films
where characters made love smoked and talked
about Mao or Sartre
playing elongated
beneath a damp sheet
bodies of desire
melt into form realms
the key is left beneath the mat

we made love
it's simple things so real
the simplest things
broken and blind
willow specific
clinging to it
this life
like and old shirt
with lost buttons and frays

threadbare body
like the life that we love

wears out
like all things

leaves of grass
mountains of stone
skin flesh and bone

the lovers I loved so much
who found me there
feeding my desire
for aspens and rivers
flowing down from the Himalayas

my passions for Bhutan
like all passions
were fulfilled
someone
and some places
in dreams
are missing
those in uniform
deformed by nightmares

In my life
I've loved them all
though some are gone
and some are missing
-Re The Beatles

In dreams I am often losing my tickets
or direction
children and luggage
days disappear
unable to find the right book
in my library

Time is not an arrow
in the peculiar presence
of my old age
as the parts start to flake away
god does not roll dice
-Re Einstein

did he say
foliation folie à deux
water flows uphill
with Jane
I know gravity is not
the weak force

all my falls tell me so

and if the big bang
of 45 magnum
universes
does not prove the mass
of light and dark matter
once existed
in one cubic centimeter

then the cosmologist of hard science
cannot think without logic
what would be the force
of that gravity
exerted on my
poor body

I enjoy the shifts
of forget me notes
and tricks of eyes
and body's desire
thrill of my lover's thighs
of juices still running

between us
in dreams
and quickie wake ups
as I spew her belly
with masses of sperm
and we giggle
well into our sixties
and now seventies
Lands of Enchantment

Peyote awakens mysteries
one of the forgotten mistresses
in the crispy vessels
of my elements

my wilted salad days
behind me

Memory plays
hide and seek
like the dock
but not tricks
in the moment
of this poem before me

I am alive
in the meadows
of timelessness
Author of Hypnerotomachia
dreaming of love with syntactic perfection

word equals all the mass
in all the universes
The journey is once
upon another time
the words were laid
and Robert Creeley said
elegant maestro
he was
to me
ever inward at Oakie Joes

"We meet in antithesis"

Was that today
I went out with you
in a morning rain

was it not rather

a year ago
or decades

lifetimes
looking for

the lapis blue Buddha

in the shadows
of
flickering
candle flicks

I reach out to
the green fields
with
the heads up to the aether

of inspired Ones
capture the

h
OM
e
in the heart
of the poem

Time like a
yellow Caterpillar
stands rusting
in the rain

soon
like this old body
nothing will remain

it is
in the
word
not the clock
or wristwatch
or the mala

syllables
make up the time
in my world

the mantras
and lyrics
the poems
the ruts left behind
by the grader

above the scrabble
of slate
broken
by years of steel
wheels
grinding

my old body
fat and weak
has nothing to do

with time

Sliding down the Rhine
I walked the halls
of Heidegger's Freiburg
in 1969
he was finishing

Being
And
Time

Sometimes in the hollow air
of Holland
art rises
like a funiculari
into a Gothic cloud
where the bride and groom
float like a fiddle

below above
in the attics
large mice loom
in the moonlight
their pink eyes
reflect

the dying ashes
in the grate

is this just my mind
traveling faster
than the speed of light

looking back over
a billion miles of life

seemingly only a day before
or this morning
before coffee
I repeat myself

Après Madam Joyce
the poet indulges in
plots
created in bed
joins the lowliest mob
protecting himself
from the contagion
of workout gyms
facial and
nail parlors
pub chatter
funereal talk
religious wars

remembering
old days in the Trieste cafe
away from the emerald skies
reflecting on a day
remembered

near the Liffey
he
always had the blues
in Autumn
stability
kind of iffy
after he turned
fifty

If Anna Livia
(the Liffey)
were not swallowed up
by the Ocean
she would certainly
debouch
into
the Canal Grande
of Trieste
had the Master
of lingo
not lived
on the Liffey
or in Trieste
the old mythology
would yet prevail
like a dagger

he even mentioned
bardo

when the deceased
passed by the pub
he rubbed
his eyes
and Bloom entered
was it before
or after
the funeral

These are the savage months
denuding trees
falling leaves

Sep
 tem ber
No
 vem ber
De
 cem ber

we all have our rivers
to remember

there was always a place
we would return to
in our memory
of sounds
and songs
carry us home

The rains fall
like blue dust
at the end of a pointed finger

pinstripes flow
along the fenders
of the candy-apple red Ford
with a big Chrysler engine
roaring past like tornados

Sixteen and cruising hard
down Colorado boulevard
my forty eight Ford
limps like humped back turtle

At six or seven
we ran behind
the DDT truck
for fun
inhaling
the sweet smelling fog
the driver
with a red bandana
waved

it is funny how kids
in innocence
are immune
to threats
and beatings

they engage in wars
of their own
dramas reenacted
from the flicks
news reels

Saturday afternoon serials
killing Japs and Nazis
with clods of earth
or Daisy air rifles

despite the dire warnings
of adults
none of us lost
an eye
we knew then
they lied
to us
about so many things
like
toads and warts
the dangers in the wood

The Alamo

the copper skinned Mexicans
from whom
huge pieces of land
larger than Europe
wrenched
from their loam filled hands

Texas later
allowed them in
to pick produce

these young natives
were my playmates
my pals
and their families
my families

unlike my own
with dramas unresolved
like players in
Eugene O'Neil's
and Tennessee's plays
wracked by histories
of family fictions
suicides and alcoholics

I lived
in a tract house
surrounded by farms
in La Ciudad
of our Lady of Angels
and these
were my friends
their families
my family
so generous in spirit
working from dawn

to sun down
in December's warm daylight

falling self
flowing
rang bop
Tibetan
syllables build my reality
a remnant of the summer gardens

in a million mantras
soft peeps of chicks
rang bop
like be bop
will the day slow
self flowing quartets in the late
afternoon

at zero we were yet infinite
running fast as we can
In the hot room where I nap
suddenly
struck by fear
threats from friends who have passed
furiously try to protect myself
arms swinging out
like a ragged boxer
Alpha touches my head
pulling me back from the dead
comfortable once again
in my cloudy bed

I turn again 'er the morn
scorpion in the east
rising with the sun
New Year's Eve

at this age I am no age
I think often of H.D.
and Virginia Woolf
all the visual realities
are like paintings
flat
with illusions of enormous depth

here I paint with
the vowels
a
e
i
o
u
and hard notes

like clang bang
rang bop

and Bebop
study the Bardo of Dying
before signing
documents
or listening to
Preachers or Fakirs

Again mass murderer kills x number of beings
Sixty Minutes interviews
Columbia psychiatrist
says fifty percent of these men have gene mishap
it runs in families
has it run there in the human genome

my only male nephew has spent his life
plagued by this disease
does anyone care
the money goes up in deformed matter
body parts with cows wheat and hookahs
exploded in billions of bombs
on perfectly healthy human beings
trapped by the monstrosity
of their possessions

OH BABY

Don't get mad at me
just because
I love your anatomy
I'm not shady or weird
there ain't nothing for you
to fear
my urges to connect are pure
even a hand job would work
for sure

Ideas in my eyes
become rationed by visions

of ordinary magnificence
the blooming of a new moon
soon to be
full
then dark
again

The stone thrown
into the air
is still for a moment
like a kite or kitten
in all things there is stillness
I am at times in meditation still

Before the wild horses of my mind
take over
nothing will stop them

Pebble or boulder also find that moment
when rolling stops
cleverness changes nothing
assumptions nor formulas
nor magic or wishes

Uncertainty Curtain
is uncertainly flowing
thru an open window
finally when I see who
was once Jack of Aces
returning from
far away places

not sure what
it all means

in his memory are spaces
as silent as that
between
thoughts
and notes
between the beats
of his big heart

Seeing Jack Hirschman
once again
in dandy clothes
Caffe Trieste
where I've hung
for 55 years

Though we romantically choose
terrible heroes
in youth
and old age
we wisely dismiss them all
at the end
of the rolling ball

a wheel in three dimensions
on a four dimensional space

clarity of thought is no thought

absolute exhaustion of all
and you sit down

eyes open into pure sky
as on high mountains
no clouds or vapors
unblinking
bindus form

the wild horses of view halted
and
busy minds are stilled

If the sun is blocked
by poison clouds
oh well

the forests of dissimilarity
bow in agony
it has happened many times
errant cosmic bodies
storms of dust
volcanic eruptions
raise dinosaur bones

they are all
just kisses
to an eternal
rebirth
of a universe insurmountable
big bang

little bang
plutonic fusions
locust

wars burying wars
bullets penetrating bullets

oh my little ones
why fret over this' and that's
keep your eye on the ball
of 108 stitches
and put down your deadly bats
How fragile the flesh and bone
rubbing against the imagination
of the moment

holding all memory
in the quick tap dancing
of afternoons passing
listening to the sounds
of infinity
sleep and wake up
dressing for the day
once again
too tired to look well
sweat pants and T shirt
my body frozen in pain
mind rushing like a flash flood
in downtown Las Vegas
America's vision of America
fucking with minds

of poor elders with a sack of dimes
at slot machines in burger joints
all the money goes
into bags
headed for the financial empires
an old Black man begs for bus money
to return to his retirement shamble
on Sepulveda Boulevard
where he will wait
for his shriveling Social Security
check

BRIDGE'N MEMORY

Memory like history
is a fiction
existing in the nothingness
of the past
yet mind of music and poesy
like fugitives flee
from the past
flooding the imagination
as my aging
becomes a playground
of degeneration
and the mind
a fugue
of exquisite confusions
slicing the moment
like a mirror
shattered

into hypnogogic shards
of a billion reflections
thrown by the sun
which still warms
my old body

and each moment
I explore the reflections
like a Bodhisattva
becoming a Bridge
of lingo
letting them all
pass over me

If you want a doctor to examine you
take my hand
I'll examine every
inch of you
I'm your man
I have walked upon the water
saying so long Maryanne
you danced me to the end of love
                -*Re: Leonard Cohen*
but the drops of me
still dribble down my thigh
have no need to get high
every disease can be eased
by the touch of you
my darling Alpha La
your wisdom fills my trunk
with a ton of honey

oh dear
I will have to leave you
someday
follow me into the lands
of another billion days
it's all for you
I have done this
and all honorable acts
the Buddha has blessed me with
just for you

You in Israel so far away
breaks my heart
and tears ripple down my cheeks
for those suffering and dying
here and there
not for bread or water
just for blood
sealing the sands of time
Sloughing off in my mind
alone in my home
with two cats
one who talks and talks
one so black
she gets lost
Confused and brilliant
in my mind
dis-eased

a musical problem
making lyrics so easy

listening to a song specific
brings tears
and heart aches
facing changes in chords and keys
for those who abide
in lyrics
they are like paint
we see in a lover's face
a smile

Who knows where the time goes
-Re Judy Collins
Making Shrines
down by the river

Namo Lu Med Ten Gyi Gonpo Lama Khyen
beyond meaning
a single syllable fills time everlasting
reveals a wisdom
hard as rock
soft as my lover's breasts
where my head lies
in sublimity
for eternity

Dakini
when we wound together
with you on top
in my lap
root erect
thousands of times

an alcoholic from the street
sleeping free above a bookstore
my wits
and alcoholic charm
kept me
out of the gutter

it was the end
or an ending of only half a life

walking the Bridge of enormous beauty
and depression
wanting to blow out my brain
so many losses
and more to come
she breathed life back into my
sweet heart
our sweat sliding
between her thigh

The tragic news comes later
on this day
Robin Williams
hangs himself
my heart broken again
how could he
I know his shoes
walked with him
into the pharmacy
that Walgreens in Laurel Village
many times

in pain and depression
we were both young then
so much left
a hundred thousand marathons
digging ditches

in our delicate hearts
joy and sorrow

both impermanent
still hurts
makes me want to

change shirts

every day

AFTERWORD

I had an early onset of dementia due to a number of reasons including polio, numerous concussions, cardiovascular disease and who knows what. It started to become apparent about ten years ago. During the writing of Section Two of this book, the disease has progressed. I am battling a rapid loss of memory but continue to do the best I can on a daily basis. But I feel so very fortunate for these 74 years of life.

As a Buddhist for nearly forty years, I have practiced and studied Dharma, and even though it is difficult to view visualizations in great depth with color, seed syllables, icons and secret mudras, I was blessed by the great compassionate Tibetan scholar and reincarnation of Guru Rinpoche himself named Dudjom Rinpoche (Jigdral Yeshe Dorje) the greatest Tibetan Scholar of the Twentieth Century and the Supreme Head of the Nyingma School of Vajrayana Buddhism. I received many empowerments, teachings and blessings (Siddhis) from His Holiness between 1976 and 1980. He passed in 1987 and on or near the time and date of his death in France, the small picture I had of him on a humble altar fell over. Called a dear friend as I believed it was a message and was told he had passed and like things had happened to many of his students around the world. My connection remains unbroken and visualizing his compassionate being has never left my heart-mind. In Tibetan, heart and mind are a single word, though there are numerous ways to explain this on outer, inner and secret levels.

Today is Sunday December 21, 2014 and exactly three years ago Dudjom's eldest son passed. He was Kabje Thinley Norbu Rinpoche. He was a supreme teacher for many Eastern and

Western Lamas, Dakas, Dakinis, advanced and ordinary students. I met him in 1976 and spent quite a lot of time with him in an ordinary way as he was not giving teachings to many Westerners at that time. On occasion, over a period of about ten years, I received profound Dzogchen teachings from him at my Buddhist Center in the Santa Cruz Mountains.

Two days after hearing of his passing my body became septic and all I could see was his passing through levels of Bardos and I thought in my half-conscious state that I was following behind him. For more than 48 hours, I was unaware of what was happening around me in an ordinary sense. My wife has been reading his newly published book "*A Brief FANTASY HISTORY of A Himalayan*" (Shambhala Press, Boston & London, 2014). Due to the prayers and blessings of many kind Lamas, Dharma friends and Sangha members, (and Western medications) I returned to good health and was given the additional time to complete this work.

> Latif Harris
> December 21, 2014
> San Francisco

"Sublime artists always give energy to others through their art. When they die, they do not leave ordinary inert substance art as a lifeless remainder, but their pure spiritual power lives in their art."

> —Kabje Thinley Norbu Rinpoche

A NOTE FROM THE EDITOR

Everything in life is so crucial, all hanging from a thread of time which we are told is only now. And yet the flood of memories takes constant stand and challenges the now and becomes inseparable. As a matter of fact 50 years ago there is a rented IBM typewriter, a Rex-Rotary mimeograph machine originally purchased from some nuns, Twiltone paper and, for me, as my part of the "mimeo revolution," a series of books/magazines called *Duende*. *Duende 12* was *Poems 1965* by William Harris, cover by artist John Czerkowicz. It was Latif's first book and, half a century gone by, *Barter Within the Bark of Trees* is his 10th book.

The joy of collating and stapling together the best little book you can and sending out copies to every poet and editor, every independent bookstore on your list, outweighed the messy task of dealing with stencils leaking ink. You did the best you could and it only cost about $25 for your supplies and $25 to mail. Others like *Wilddog, Desperado, Olé, Sum, Grand Ronde Review, Litmus, Desert Review, Blitz, Wormwood, Renegade, Imago, Second Coming* then appeared as exchanges in your mailbox. It was poet-controlled publishing as only now we're seeing it again in Publish On Demand.

Latif brought to us his very early 60's North Beach experiences of Auerhahn Press people, Robert LaVigne, John Wieners, Phillip Lamantia, as well as his experience starting *Ante Magazine* in Los Angeles. His California sensibility was welcome and energizing here in Albuquerque-Placitas. Both of us were under the New Mexico teaching aura of Robert Creeley, both of us sharing the grace of poetry. It was an emotional friendship with local poets and painters making up the venue. The brilliant British novelist Ann Quin was living here as was David Franks, Kell Robertson, and Bill Pearlman, and then Judy Grahn. My first book *Cycles* (1964) came about because Latif edited down my voluminous 60's outpouring. I am so grateful for that and our continuing friendship. Life has thrown us both passages of intense importance but we haven't lost our connection.

Coyote Seen, Beneath the Wheel (Selected Poems 1963-1983), and the supreme pizzazz and true Buddhist energy of *A Bodhisattva's Busted Truth* remain close to me, as well as his massive compilation, along with Neeli Cherkovski, of *The Beatitude Golden Anniversary 1959-2009*. *Barter Within the Bark of Trees* now presents us beautifully a voice of maturity and soul.

Larry Goodell / Duende Press / Placitas, New Mexico

BOOKS BY AUTHOR

Editor **CITADEL** literary magazine L.A. City College 1962

Founding Editor/Publisher of **ANTE** literary magazine Los Angeles 1963

POEMS 1965 Duende Press, New Mexico 1965

Editor **THUNDERBIRD** literary magazine UNM Albuquerque, NM 1966

MOUNTAIN SCRIPTS Mill Valley, CA 1974

JOURNEY TO THE MOON Celestial Arts Millbrae, CA 1974

A POWER SET APART Celestial Arts Millbrae, CA 1975

ANTI OBJECTS Vorpal Gallery San Francisco, CA 1979

BENEATH THE WHEEL Selected Poems Des Pair Press San Francisco 1983

COYOTE SEEN Deep Forest San Francisco, CA 1992

AUTOTOXAEMIA Deep Forest San Francisco, CA 1993

AFTERNOON OF POETRY Alpha Gardner San Francisco, CA 1993

LIFEWORKS Selected Poems *1958-2005* (special edition 108 copies in conjunction with gallery show of authors art works) Cogswell College Sunnyvale, CA 2005

BODHISATTVA'S BUSTED TRUTH Browser Books San Francisco, CA 2006

Editor/Publisher **BEATITUDE GOLDEN ANNIVERSARY** San Francisco 2009

BARTER WITHIN THE BARK OF TREES Duende Press, NM 2015

First Edition
500 copies printed paper
With 26 lettered copies hardbound with jacket
Signed by Author

Duende Press

Placitas, New Mexico

165 M Ave
98 Oakland Ca
94603